DELIUS KLASING

ZH·487 489

EDL 756C

BOX on Wheels

Extraordinary VW Camper Vans

Norbert Nettekoven

Delius Klasing Verlag

Contents

6

20

28

38

44

60

90

114

130

Stretchness

YUMOSVW

Melina and Kevin found Fiona in Central Washington, where the stretch limo had been used as a mobile bakery. „We pulled it from where it had sat for about 10 years outside, with holes in the ceiling and totally ransacked. Over the course of the project many friends helped me, such as a surfboard shaper with the fiberglass work, my girlfriend with the upholstery, and a woodworker friend helped me create the interior I'd designed," says Kevin.

Fiona – air-cooled through the Black Hills

„We now run Fiona as a tour company bus in the Black Hills of South Dakota. While Fiona takes some love to keep on the road, she is quite easy to drive and actually gets blown around on the road less than my regular buses due to the tandem rear axle. She is powered by a 2332 cc custom made engine with a full flow oil cooler. I've gone almost 80 in her before, though typically with people I stay at much slower speeds. She has brakes to all six wheels and tandem e-brakes to both rear axles. This past year we did nearly 12,000 miles of tours with her and I can proudly say she made it back to her garage every trip this past season!" says Kevin.

Fiona the DubBus
Black Hills Tour Co.

ENGINE	2332 CC CUSTOM
LENGTH	SUFFICIENT
SEATS	12
SHE NO LONGER LIKES	BAKERS
HER DREAM	DRIVE HARD ROCK BANDS TO THEIR GIGS

Five at one stroke

When a stretch limo is based on an old VW bus of the T3 range, the chauffeur and the passengers can be sure of drawing the undivided attention of passers-by. It took 3,000 man hours and a total of five transporters to create this exclusive and unique specimen with three axles, all done in the garage „Die Werkstatt" of VW transporter specialists Christian Lemke and Stefan Schreiber in Berlin.

www.bulli -limo.de

The standard engine was replaced with a modern 180 hp V6 diesel engine from a VW Passat. Several reinforcements prevent the bodywork from sagging. The cockpit was enhanced with a handmade dashboard modelled from two Passat cockpits. Newly upholstered and covered seats as well as exquisite materials create a luxurious atmosphere also in the chauffeur's cabin. A fold-out screen allows him to monitor the passenger compartment at all times. Various LED spotlights and chains of lights as well as a hand-crafted starry sky with glass fibre optics can also be controlled from the driver's seat.

The side sliding door has been extended to a length of 2.5 metres for easy access, while the huge sunroof creates a sense of well-being. A 47 inch flat screen TV is integrated in the front area, to either watch telly or indulge in computer games with a Playstation 3. A total of twelve Rainbow loudspeakers and two large subwoofers powered by four amplifiers in the rear are the ingredients for an amazing sound system. A real eye-catcher.

Luise

ENGINE	180 HP, V6
AXLES	3
LENGTH	8.5 M
TV	47 INCH
BOOKABLE:	STOP-AND-SEARCH
	OPERATION BY A STRIPPER

Monorail Station
SIR JOHN YOUNG HOTEL
Anzac Bridge

„The project took about 2 years to source all the parts and materials," says Sean. He was very meticulous about retaining the original concept styling on the outside, but adding special finishes and details on the inside to produce what is a tremendous eye catching looking limousine.It was a magnificent feat of engineering made from one Kombi only with thousands of man hours! Totally Australian made.

A first in Australia

Sean Devine loves Kombis and one day he decided to produce a fully customized VW limousine. He bought a 1962 Kombi in a very sad state in Canberra and took it to Riverstone to cut it in half. Side panels were made from sheet metal: cut, shaped, welded and added to form the stretched body. „We needed something nice to push the car along when you have 10 people in the back", says Sean and put a V6 in the rear.

Kombi Limousines
Sidney, Sean Devine

YEAR	1962
ENGINE	2.5 LV6 TURBO
AXLES	2
LENGTH	6.3 M
TV	4 X 43 INCH
FULL LENGTH SUNROOF	

Keller-Bert's Stretch

Bernd Mossmann, nicknamed Keller-Bert, loves fresh fruit and vegetables. He has created a storage room between the longitudinal chassis beams in the basement of his Kombi, which keeps the supplies cool and appetizing. In order to be able to stash enough provisions on longer journeys, he somewhat extended the bus, mounted another rear axle and fitted all spoilers manually. At the rear, a six-cylinder engine is at work generating enough air to cool the storage cellar. Bernd and his colleagues from the VW Bus Team Baden are interested in tuning, but also spend a lot of time keeping their Kombis in their original condition and are strictly against scrapping bonuses.

Keller-Bert's Stretch
Bernd Mossmann

ENGINE	VR6
AXLES	3
CELLAR	1
IS PROUD OF	MANUALLY FITTED SPOILERS, PASSED TECHNICAL INSPECTION

Stretch Samba
Bob van Heyst

YEAR	1962
AXLES	2
EXTRAS	SUNROOF, SAFARI WINDOWS, BLAUPUNKT RADIO

The Long Belgian

In 1986, Arlette van Dijck und Bob van Heyst founded BBT on 20 m², today they have 4,000 m², 20 employees and established themselves in the Kombi scene with sound advice, excellent service and a wide range of spare parts. Bob collects VW cars, rare steering wheels, small parts and radios for Split Window Beetles – and occasionally he extends black/red Kombis!

YUMOSVW

In 2013, the last of over one million T2 transporters was produced in Brazil. Since 1997, Yumo's garage in Semarang, Indonesia, has been converting used Brazilian T2 models with eight windows into brand new looking busses with a T1 look – with 11, 15 or more windows. Yumo delivers worldwide. Be it a camper, standard or classy construction, everything is possible and manual work guaranteed.

Indonesian tin artists

Yumo's garage bears his signature and even before you enter you can tell he's a staunch Kombi fan. Above the entrance, half a T1 sticks out of the wall, there are VW emblems all over the place, sales counters are made of Kombi fronts, bricks have been cast with the VW logo and bus fragments built into the wall – visitors are immediately tuned in. Here, buses are restored or extended and built with 23 windows and more. On the Internet and social media platforms, Yumo demonstrates what he and his team have to offer. Restorations, conversions, snail campers, patina'd custom-made designs and artistic aluminium bodywork. Yumo's artists will also happily use classic icon cars such as the Porsche 356 and clone them entirely from aluminium. Sometimes the original spare parts do not fit anymore, because everything is rebuilt by hand, which is why parts from other manufacturers are occasionally installed. But without doubt, the focus here is undoubtedly on the enthusiasm and virtuosity of the constructors and not on obtaining European road approval.

Stretch Replica Yumo's Garage

TYPE	1980 KOMBI BRAZIL
ENGINE	ORIGINAL
AXLES	3
LENGTH	7.60 M
SKYLIGHTS	18

Shortness

Frosty

Billo loves the design simplicity of classic VWs. „Detroit is a very competitive market for all types of automobiles and, of course, American-made cars rule the roost. I believe it was a very big deal for the Short Bus to be accepted in the local car culture so positively," enthuses Billo.

The tiny VW bus is an eye-catcher, makes minds boggle and brings a smile to everybody's face. Billo's trick: The Short Bus is perfectly proportioned, shortened by two feet, lowered by 10" and running on low profile Yokohama S-Drive 205/50/R16's. „I'm 6'4" and weigh 300 lbs. So when I climb out of it, it just blows people's minds!" says Bill with a smile.

Billo's Detroit Shorty

„Sometimes people ask me if it's a new model VW has come out with! Go figure!" laughs Billo. „That said, when I got it, it wasn't the most mechanically sound and trustworthy vehicle to drive. It „looked good", but had been sorely neglected mechanically. I considered it a diamond in the rough...to put it mildly. The bones were there, but it needed a lot of help. So that's what I did. I helped it become what it is today. It's a very cool, tiny VW bus that fools the eye and brings a smile to your face! You can't ask for anything more than that." Bill got a lot of help from the Detroit automotive scene. The body has been shortened by 2 feet. Except for the custom safari window on the rear hatch, all safari and hinged windows are original and only tinted. „Sometimes I think I'm done, but since 2011 I keep having new ideas. Oh yeah! I also had „THE SHORT BUS" machined in stainless steel, and replaced the „VOLKSWAGEN" script on the rear of the bus with it." „Tiny cool" down to the last detail.

Billo's Short Bus

ENGINE	120 HP CUSTOM
LENGTH	MINUS 60 CM
HEIGHT	MINUS 20 CM
SOULMATE	DANNY DEVITO (1.47 M)
SHORTY'S DREAM	SMALL TRAILER, MAX. 80 CM

The VW bus enjoys continuing popularity worldwide and irrespective of any technical feasibility, ideas for the most bizarre rebuilds emerge. For such a car to be recognized later as a VW bus, it is sometimes only necessary to preserve the characteristic elements of the T1, the lateral strips running together at the front to form a large „V" and the surrounding roof edge.

Shortened wheelbases and often a high engine power would lift up the front wheels of some Shorties at full throttle. Support wheels at the rear, like on skateboards, prevent this. Bizarre car bodies, sheet-metal cartoons between comic strip and high-tech. Some may find the original headlight housings of the VW T1 too dainty and will replace them with shiny chrome salad bowls.

Instead of the standard 1,500 air boxer with 42 hp and 95.1 Newton metres, a real power pack is at work in some Shorties: 2.2 litres four-cylinder engines with dual carburettors and ceramic-coated headers delivering up to 330 hp. At a weight of less than one tonne, the power-to-weight ratio is equal to that of a Porsche 911 GT3. A heavy burden on the support wheel.

The results are often reminiscent of Hot Wheels model cars from the 1970s or of Fillmore from the Pixar film „Cars". Anything is permitted with the Shorty. Here the Kombi becomes a magic cube with millions of possible combinations. The Kombi has not only become one of the most iconic cars of the 20th century, it is also easy to pimp. And no matter what, it's always lovable.

Lowness

WAY OUT

Harvey had seen the Splitty at a VW show on Santa Pod Raceway and knew he had to have such a perfectly patina'd bus. When he heard that you can't fit 17x7 American Racing Torque Thrust wheels on a Splitty front axle, Harvey turned to Paul and his experienced team at Type2Detectives for advice at the recommendation of Stance|Works. Lowering the bus was only the beginning...

Splitty Wants To Eat Floor

The classic bench seat was re-wrapped in a rich brown baseball glove leather and the rear cargo area was given a new canvas top. With fender work also came a custom inner beam from T2D, and a fancy Rayvern hydraulics kit for the front end. Future plans are a 2.2 l engine from a Porsche or a Fastroad Type , along with a matching set of hydros for the rear of the truck. Such stories never really end.

Type 2 Detectives

TYPE	FLATBED TRUCK
COLOUR	PATINA'D
FRONT	RAYVEM HYDRAULICS KIT
HE LOVES	68 DODGE CHARGER
	(SAME SIZE OF SHOES)

PILOT
Cool Rydes
TURBINE INTAKE
COOLING
PHOENIX
F/X

This was a design concept Kevin „CoolRydes" Zagar had been thinking about for many years. He had seen how people can get enthusiastic about the Bus Drag Race. Kombi fans or not, everyone was amused at the idea of an old, slow bus participating in a race and no one believed that it could be done head held high. Then came Kevin and his crew.

The Top Gun Drag Bus

Kevin had promised the organizers of the famous „Elite and Just Clean VW Show" in Las Vegas to deliver such a vehicle within only 15 days of construction time. There is nothing more to be said: Kevin drummed up friends and employees and challenged his luck. With tuning experience and motivated guys behind him, the Drag Bus could be loaded on time after 15 days at 4:30 in the morning, and Kevin and his crew left for Las Vegas, tired but happy. During these 15 days, a 1957 car body was mounted on a 1969 chassis with a fully nickel-plated Mendeola suspension. CoolStop disc brakes with Wilwood callipers on all four wheels give the 10.5" Phoenix slicks braking power. To get this baby down the strip in Vegas, she has an ARPM block, Deano Dyno-Soars Super Flo cylinder heads, crowned with a turbo, powered by a Holley 650 dual carburetor and a Rancho Pro Street transmission system. That sounds wild and guarantees more fun than is allowed. Kevin's motto: "We love to live in this world of unlimited possibilities - so anything is possible."

Top Gun Drag Bus
Kevin »CoolRydes« Zagar

YEAR	1957 / 1969
ENGINE	CUSTOM
	TURBOCHARGED
POWER	SUFFICIENT
SHOES	PHOENIX DRAG SLICKS

Kester's Volkswagenwerks

If you're on the Route 66 in Arizona going through Holbrook, by the roadside you'll see a number of old and modified VWs scattered somewhat randomly about the premises of „Kester's Volkswagenwerks". Not as famous as some other „Mother Road" attractions, but the VW Bug reference in this area. In the past, when a VW Beetle was still on a high pole on the side of the road, pointing the way for travellers, they also sold petrol here. Earl Kester's pride and joy was the opening of his own store in 1988. Though retired, he still enjoys his VWs and his job as treasurer of the Route 66 Gearheads Car Club.

Instead of converting the 1963 VW bus into a motorhome, Mike „Hotrod" Rowan shares his Splitty with a 586 hp 7.7 litre Big Block Chevy V8.

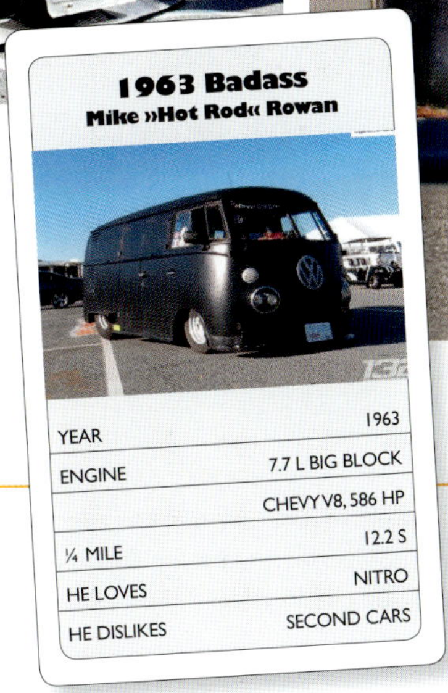

1963 Badass

Mike bought the abandoned bus which was standing on a field in Georgia for $275, and it took only six weeks to create this Badass. Of course Mike also uses it for his daily inner-city trips, a second car is out of the question. If 586 hp is not enough, he still has 150 nitro shots up his sleeve. Mike covers the quarter mile in 12.2 seconds.

Service

It all began in 1972 as a VW Type 2 low-loader platform truck and ended with a tandem axle in sunny California. After its work stay in the USA, the flatbed vehicle found its way back to Europe, where it was completely restored by Kieft & Klok in Holland. When carrying a Porsche or VW bus, it still hits just over 110 km/h! The pastel blue is absolutely authentic, they even thought of matching door stickers.

Speedy Transport

As early as 1950, Volkswagen informed its dealers and customers of the wide range of special models in the brochure „Speedy Transport"; the market niche was found! Shortly after the introduction of the flatbed truck in 1952, it was merrily rebuilt, raised, extended and lowered. A pure work tool at the time, today the pleasure begins on the trip to the show when a suitable Porsche 356 is piggybacked.

»Speedy Transport«
Kieft & Klok

YEAR	1972 FLATBED WITH WINCH AND TANDEM AXLE, 1,700 KG PAYLOAD
ENGINE	2 L, 68 HP
HE LOVES	PORSCHE 356
HE DISLIKES	RED FERRARIS

Liftness

P·E·A·C·E

Twist of Fate

School busses make you think back to wild and easy-going schooldays. Their shape and coulour are iconic and they smell of school. Retired school buses can be found as guest rooms behind grandpa's house, colourful elements in the street food scene and mobile homes for hikers who don't really want to leave their home. And some people can't choose between a Volkswagen motorhome and a school bus. So why not glue a Kombi to a school bus? Michael Divine, a Californian artist, painted a bus. Not just any bus – it bears the name „Twist of Fate". „It was a pretty wild thing, several layers, velvet upholstery, embroidery, a sound system. I showed up without a plan and only had a vague idea. I decided to let the inner character of the bus shine through to the outside. A neat piece of work," says Michael.

Twist of Fate

ARTWORK	MICHAEL DIVINE
CAN BE SEEN IN	SAN DIEGO, CA
SCHOOL BUS	FORD B-SERIES
GUESTROOM	SPLITTY
HE LOVES	BURNING MAN FESTIVAL NEVADA

Sax Gordon

„I don't know the owner, but I was told that a group of artists was on the road with this Skooly," says Gordon Beadle a.k.a. „Sax Gordon", charismatic saxophone virtuoso, who sent us this picture from Worcester, MA. The painting and the brushed-on slogans like „Let the sunshine in", „Love, Peace, 100 smiles" and the portraits of Jimi Hendrix and Jim Morrison on the fender all point to old hippies or their children or grandchildren.

A motorhome with a fireplace, second-hand wood panelling, a piano, a kitchen, a veranda and a picket fence? Equipment which is rarely found in mobile homes. For the two musicians Dave Weaver and Thomas Rumble from Austin TX, this unorthodox American dream is reality. After graduating from college, they wanted to build a motorhome that was both unique and environmentally friendly.

Magic bus

On the roof of the 1979 Bluebird International school bus which the two bought for little money, they grafted a T2 Westfalia camper penthouse whose rear hatch allows access the spacious sun terrace. The RV was embellished with a 1960s hippie paintwork in blue and orange. Under the bonnet a modified diesel engine develops sufficient torque with used vegetable oil. The Magic Bus burns 33 l per 100 km and after a while it occasionally reaches 90 km/h on a straight stretch. Chip fat is stored in three 190 l tanks, one tank is filled with diesel just in case. The Skooly movement was born in the USA, where these vehicles are popular as a base for motorhomes due to their simple mechanics, robustness and length. Once the passenger seats have been removed, you have a space of up to 22 square metres. „It's good to drive, but you feel every pothole, the glasses rattle and you think the fridge is about to fall out. It's not suitable for offroad adventures. In city traffic, you can't get the Skooly around the corner at times and have to back up much to the annoyance of the person behind you."

Magic Bus

SCHOOLBUS	1979 BLUEBIRD INT.
GUESTROOM	WESTFALIA CAMPER
BEDS	6
HE LOVES	CHIP FAT
HE DISLIKES	NARROW BENDS
RULE NO. 1	SHOES OFF PLEASE!

Family Bus-iness

Dometic

One day Jeremiah Luce, his wife and two teenage daughters, Charity (15) and Ella (13), packed up their lives and moved into the bus. They did not renew the lease for their house, sold off some of their belongings and took to the road. Since then, they've been to almost every state and put 20,000 miles on that bus, which itself runs on vegetable oil.

Road Sweet Home – The Bus Family

Jeremiah cut a VW van in two and welded the upper half on top of the school bus to make the youngsters' bedroom. The family spends time at different state parks and farms, volunteering in communities as a form of barter. „There's no hidden trust fund for this," says Jeremiah, „ Every now and then someone will look at us like we're super sketchy. Doesn't matter, it's all cool. Our lifestyle operates on a belief that joy is the true currency. And life is short."

Kushti Bok – Gypsies in Australia

Gypsy Love and Max Flint have been living in their 1974 Kombi for many years roaming Australia. They sell jewellery and fill their tank with fortune telling and their fridge with healing workshops. As is customary for travelling people, they head for markets, fairs and festivals. Gypsy also knows how to capture orbs in photos. Orbs look like little circles of light, but they are actually ghosts that surround us.

The Tiki Hut
Molly, Ron & Wylder

TYPE	SPLITTY
TECHNOLOGY	DROPPED, WORKS
FAN OF	HAWAII FIVE-O
SHE NO LONGER LIKES	HAWAIIAN SHIRTS
HER DREAM	GO TO HAWAII FOR THE IRON MAN WC

Ron Bureta's Tiki Hut

Tiki arose in the USA during the Exotica wave of the 1950s and continues to be the embodiment of South Pacific romance, wreaths of flowers and glowing sunsets. In the Western USA, Molly, Ron and Wylder are constantly dreaming of this in their Kombi under the self-constructed bamboo tiki roof. Aloha!

Dometic

„**My daughter Kenzie** is my co-pilot on every tour and has been with me from the start. Kenzie named our 1971 T2 simply „The Bus". The best part of our VW life is the people we meet on our trips. Everyone has a father, uncle, cousin or friend who also has a Kombi. Everywhere I stop, someone has a little story to tell about a Kombi and wants to share it with us," says Victor Melendez from Florida.

The Bus

To fit the big tyres, Victor's bus was raised a little bit. It looks rough, but thanks to power steering and Koni dampers, it drives nice and smoothly. At the moment The Bus has an air-cooled 1,600 cc engine, but Victor is thinking about a diesel conversion. Inside there is a TV, Blue Ray, sound bar, stove, fridge, LED lights, a porta potty for Kenzie and a bed. Of course, in sunny Florida, Victor can easily generate electricity with a 300 watt Renogy solar panel system powered by lithium batteries. But just in case he has a 3 kW generator on the bumper. „We've been driving our bus for five years now and had a lot of fun together. Bus is a family member, we worry when he's sick and then treat him to a hand wash," says Victor. At the Florida Bug Jam, The Bus even won the first prize in the Total Conversion category.

On a sunny Albuquerque afternoon, Nancy und Mark Wall found a trashed out, beat-up 1961 Westphalia bus which was due to be crushed for scrap that very afternoon. After some haggling, Nancy purchased the wreck for $113. „We called it `the little bus that nobody wanted´."

It has taken years of work using miles of thread, fabric, tapestries, beads, lights, crystals, tassels and gallons of hot glue and liquid nails to produce this beautiful bus. „'The Genie Bottle' is a work of art, but still retains ist 'VW BUS-NESS' and is a fully stocked, working camper. It has become our hobby, therapy and artistic outlet," says Nancy Wall.

The Genie Bottle

„As a kid, my family travelled Route 66 in a decked-out shiny red and white Westfalia camper. In 1973, as newlyweds, we bought our first VW. We almost wore out a 'VW Manual Repair Guide for the Complete Idiot' rebuilding engines and keeping our VWs alive and well," recalls Nancy. In 1999, they were looking for a more comfortable camping setup in the form of a water bed. Mark gutted the bus, including the rotting 1960s Chevy truck bucket seats and the vintage 1970s rust coloured shag rug that had been glued to the whole interior. With a sledgehammer and tin snips I made room for a steel frame to hold the water bed. Meanwhile, Nancy emptied 400 bottles of glitter nail polish to paint the car body. „We left our first VW show with a trophy for best interior and inspiration to continue decorating. We gave 'The Genie Bottle' a new life and saved her from the scrap press. We share her with the fans, but we will never sell her. She is a work of art, reminiscent of our 1960s hippie years."

The Genie Bottle
Nancy & Mark Wall

YEAR	1961 CAMPER VAN
TECHNOLOGY	WATER BED
SHE NO LONGER LIKES	NAIL POLISH
HER DREAM	LARGE MIRROR BALL

Romina (28) and Martín (26) from Córdoba, Argentina, are building 'Frankie' for the trip of their dreams. „It comes from Frankenstein, because the bus is made up of Volkswagen, Fiat, Toyota, Ford, Hyundai and Rover parts. We'll travel the American continent with it, from Ushuaia, the southernmost city in the world, all the way to Alaska. We have decided to do things that do us good," says Martin.

Frankie goes Alaska – viviendo caminos

The Panamericana stretches north to south across the whole American continent. 19 different states, many climate zones, dense jungle and high mountain passes have to be crossed. Frankie has a 120 hp dohc Fiat engine behind the front seats, differentials and front axle are from a Ford Ranger, the rear leaf springs from a Toyota Hilux. Martín loves his „transplants" and finds that he collects from friends and car cemeteries. It's not only a trip for Romina and Martín, it's a new way of life that they dream of. „We have a mobile workbench to produce key fobs made of recycled materials when we're on the road. We want to travel slowly and relaxed and reach the northernmost point of our continent in two years' time," says Martín. His Frankie is still under construction and will definitely be on the road soon. Have a safe journey! Por un nuevo estilo de vida!

Frankie
Romina and Martín

YEAR	1980
MANUFACTURERS	VW AND 6 OTHERS
POWER	120 HP
FRANKIE LIKES	MARTIN'S FIRST
	DRAFT OF FRANKIE
FRANKIE DISLIKES	CAR WASHES

During the Christmas season, the families of the „505 VW Bus Club" decorate their Kombis for the annual Twinkle Light Parade in Albuquerque, New Mexico. For days on end, thousands of LEDs and twinkling lights are painstakingly glued to the bus to create a unique spectacle on wheels.

„**When we see** the children by the roadside waving with excitement, we know that we have done something right," says Alfonso Garcia Jr. about his blinking bus. „It's turned into a family tradition. For us the VW Kombi has a personality and we let it speak for itself. Everything is DIY, nothing is out of the catalogue."

Twinkle Light Parade in New Mexico

„**It started six years ago** with about 450 lights on my bus. This year I decorated my bus with ten times as many lights which took me six hours. But I forget about all the work when I see smiling faces all over the world," says Garcia. His latest videos got millions of views on YouTube. „We can reach a large group of people and make them happy. People write to us from Scotland, Puerto Rico and Germany." After the Parade, the 505 VW Bus crew helps Santa Claus give out Christmas presents in the children's hospital. „Children don't deserve to be sick at Christmas and not be with their families. If a toy or a furry friend can bring a moment of happiness, we are all ready to help. Take a minute and think about how rich we all are. It's much easier to be humble when you know what it really means to have a hard time," says Garcia.

505 VW Bus
Alfonso Garcia jr.

HOME	ALBUQUERQUE, NM
LED LIGHTS	5,900
THEY ALL LIKE	FAMILY TRIPS
	TWINKLE LIGHT PARADE
	KIDS

„Father and Son“ are well-known German cartoon figures. The pantomime comic depicts a father and his son grappling with various everyday situations and finding unusual solutions for them. That's what Frank Kutheus found for his T1 flatbed father and his little son on quad wheels.

Father and Son

The car body for the son comes from Belgium. To help him learn to walk, Frank put him on an invalid car with an electric drive which meant low torque and long loading times. For an adolescent this doesn't exactly rock, so in 2015 the son got a 50 cc engine and the rear axle of a quad. We are curious to see what „Grandfather Frank“ will come up with when the little one will be going into puberty soon.

Fancyness

O NORDESTE

Forró is a traditional genre of Brazilian music and the most popular dance for couples in Brazil. It is currently experiencing a worldwide boom. With his 1973 VW Bus, Cacai Nunes delivers the music to go with these flowing and harmonious movements, only from records, of course.

For 16 years, Cacai Nunes, musician, guitarist, researcher, producer and DJ, has been exploring and preserving the traditional music of his native Brazil, especially the north-eastern Brazilian Forró tradition. Cacai has a huge vinyl collection and with this treasure he wanted to make people dance in many different places all over the country.

Forró de Vitrola – Brazilian Vinyl

He dreamt of a car that evokes the same historical associations as his repertoire of records from the 50s, 60s and 70s. „Then I saw an abandoned, completely dilapidated 1973 VW bus and imagined how it would be the highlight of every party, beautifully repainted with turntables, sound and lighting. I put my dream into practice and now my Kombi is my key to mobility. On squares, at village festivals and trade fairs, in museums and train stations I can open the roof and get started. I have all the necessary equipment for the dance on board. I'm proud of my own cultural equipment that can carry me everywhere and allows me to keep this great tradition alive," says Cacai. I have also reached the musicians of the new generation and they try to interpret these old songs, and that way the work of those musicians finds its way back into the musical cycle. Cacai and his VW partner certainly got the ball rolling.

www.dub-box.com
VNP 804L

Dub Box was born out of necessity. An ever-growing family and only a split screen camper! Matt Clay needed a cool and affordable solution. It had to be light enough to be towed by his 48 horse powered camper, but would need to look cool. Insulation with the British climate would be imperative, as well as finding the right repro fixtures and fittings that would ensure the aesthetics would be spot on.

Dub Box Retro Camper

Taking inspiration from American classic caravans, two back ends of front-end crashes were moulded into a fibreglass shell. Fitted on a BPW braked T section chassis – and Dub Box was born. Dub Box can be colour matched to your towing vehicle and customers choose their own upholstery, kitchen cupboards, worktops, flooring and blinds. Dub Box is a trailer that really puts the cool back into caravaning.

Dub Box Retro Camper

ENGINE	2 OR 4 BEDS
WEIGHT	590 TO 1,300 KG
CHASSIS	BPW, BRAKED
COMES AS	CAMPER, SHORTY, SALAD BAR, COCKTAIL BAR, ICE CREAM PARLOUR

Many years ago, Dave Manning quit his job and started living on the road full time as a musician. He's living his dream and has many stories to tell. „I like to think I'm an artist, following his heart, even if to some I'm just the weirdo living in his van down by the river," smiles Dave.

Blues Vincent

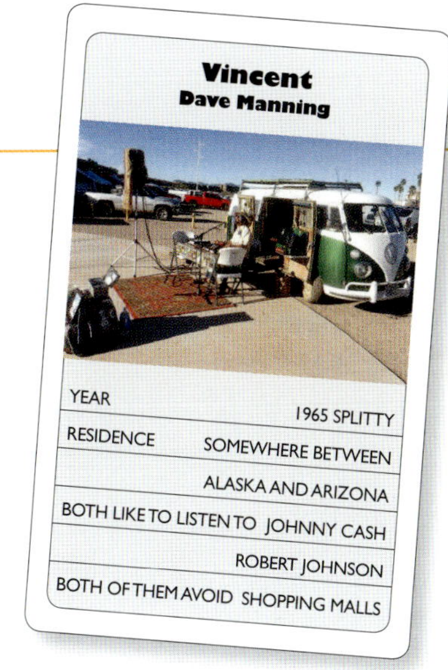

„I bought my VW bus when I was 17 and I've been driving „Vincent" ever since. I guess I missed the consumerism memo that says we're supposed to buy a new car every few years. I play what I like to call a „Roots Blues Review". In addition to my own songs, I'll be playing the classics from Leadbelly and Robert Johnson to Jerry Lee Lewis and Johnny Cash - artists that drew their music from the blues." Dave Manning has been touring North America for years. In a time when the travelling storytellers and songwriters have long been replaced by television and Karaoke, Dave is still out there with the last of them. Cruising at a lazy 50mph and playing in a different town every few days, his bus is full of stories. Dave says: „I map my tours out by where I have good friends, where the land is beautiful and where the good hotsprings are. I stay out west where you still have big spaces, few shopping malls and I'm more likely to hold a conversation with a wild horse or a lizard."

Ben Levy from Oldbury, West Midlands, has a thriving bicycle shop and had less and less time to make it down the pub to meet his friends for a beer. Therefore, he decided to help himself and in painstaking detail work he turned a VW van into an authentic British pub.

Ben's air-cooled pub is called „The Dub Inn", an allusion to the Kombi nickname „Vdub". It is equipped with a counter, red upholstered pub seats, bottle shelves and even a dartboard. Like the real thing it has brass beer taps, wooden wine shelves, disco lights and a bell for service.

The Dub Inn

Ben had seen the Canadian VW bus at a car show and spontaneously decided to buy it. „In fact I had no idea what to do with it. A friend of mine said, a pub in a bus would be something else. I'd never seen anything like it and I thought - why not? Then I would have my own pub and my own opening times," he says with a smile. There's not a lot of space in the Dub Inn, but it's cosy, up to four people can squeeze in and there's even room for a few drinks left. Volkswagen vans have a very large fan base in England, and the Dub Inn is absolutely British and very well known by now. Ben and his mates always enjoy a beer and a game of darts by the roadside or in front of his house. But Ben emphasizes that after a few beers, needless to say, he doesn't drive anymore.

The Dub Inn
Ben Levy

YEAR	1965
COMES	FROM CANADA
RESIDENCE	OLDBURY,
	WEST MIDLANDS, GB
HE LOVES	RED UPHOLSTERY,
	BRASS, DARTS

Bliss n Eso Custom Kombi

This is not just any old Boombox. The idea was that the hip hoppers from Bliss n Eso drive onto the stage in the bus, start spinning their decks, pump up the grooves and pull off the whole live show without the DJ leaving the vehicle.

BNE 28

After four years of construction, the band Bliss n Eso officially presented their 1976 VW Kombi Type 2 at the MotorEX in Melbourne in 2014. The green masterpiece is the centre of their stage show. „We've had this dream for ten years and when we drove on stage for the first time and the audience went crazy, it was a very moving moment for us," says Jonathan Notley a.k.a. „MC Bliss".

In the centre of the stage at the *Circus Under The Stars Tour*

Built by „Brothers Speed Shop" on the Australian Gold Coast, the Kombi tours as a unique showcar with a customized DJ console as well as a special audio and video system and is an integral part of the stage show. From the custom-made electric roof to the air suspension system and the handmade chassis rails, everything was rebuilt, not leaving out the original headlights, handles and windows.

Bliss n Eso Custom Kombi

YEAR	1976 BLISS N ESO
CONSTRUCTION TIME	4 YEARS
POWER	24 LOUDSPEAKERS, 4 SUBWOOFERS, 8 AMPLIFIERS
GODFATHERS	BROTHERS SPEED SHOP, J. NOTLEY & L. DORING

PIZZA PICKUP
AUTHENTIC ITALIAN WOODFIRED PIZZA
WWW.PIZZAPICKUP.CO.UK
PIZZA PICKUP
PIZZA
PICKUP
WWW.PIZZAPICKUP.CO.UK

After many years on the road as a hardworking double cab pickup truck, it finally came to a halt in front of 64 Peckham Rye as the absolute star of the Pizza Pickup team. With a special pizza oven designed in 1503, Nico met the taste of the people in the London district of Peckham. The Kombi is authentic, the pizza has a thin base, thin crust, is fired with wood only and brought to absolute perfection.

Woodfired pizza from the crew cab

Nicos woodfired pizza had something to celebrate in 2017: 50,000 pepperoni pizzas in and out of the oven. That doesn't impress the Double Cab, it has covered several 100,000 km. In case of a special event, Pizza Pickup will also come to your home. Up to 60 people can be served without any problem. Molto bene ragazza.

AL-42-02

As early as the beginning of the 1950s, VW and Westfalia offered sales car conversions with side flaps hinged at the top. Usually, the conversions were based on vans with a central corridor so that the sales area could be accessed from the driver's cab. Mobile post offices, banks, ice cream parlours, bakeries and groceries appeared – in short: everything the customer desired in the period of economic boom.

Barbus

At the request of the customer, this 1967 transporter was turned into a Barbus with an opening roof by Kieft&Klok in Holland. The bus was completely overhauled and after extensive welding work it was converted into a mobile bar. Now it has a folding roof and a counter. Rather than a grey-frocked retailer selling his goods, professional bar staff, flair bartenders and baristas give the bus a retro feel.

Barbus
Kieft & Klok, NL

YEAR	1967 / 1,600 CC
COLOURS	L360 AQUAMARINE,
	L680 CUMULUS WHITE
HE LOVES	BLUE CURACAO
HE DISLIKES	DRIZZLE

VW Büssli from the Internet

A private seller in the USA had put up the 1966 T1 bus for sale on the Internet. Apparently it was in excellent condition. A Kombi fan from Zurich went for it and had a rusty surprise in Rotterdam.

ZH·487 489

ZH·487 489

Raphael Sommer from Switzerland bought a 1966 T1 on the Internet from the USA. The vehicle was supposed to be in perfect condition, the photos looked fine. But this turned out to be fake news. The undercarriage was like a sieve, and any hope of a speedy restoration died when after the first sandblasting the whole disaster came to light. „The sides looked like they'd had an encounter with Al Capone's machine gun," says Raphael, still getting angry at the thought today. Scrap yard or a life's work? He decided to go for the full monty and contacted coachbuilders, engine specialists, saddlers and carpenters for the interior fittings. After many months and around 1,600 working hours, he had turned it into an absolute beauty. By chance, the story continued in Northern Germany, where a used Westfalia camping trailer was on offer. This time Raphael inspected it personally, approved and bought it. This Westfalia trailer 310/4 is a rarity and, like the bus, dates back to 1966.

Büssli

YEAR	1966
POWER	44 HP
CONSTRUCTION TIME	2 YEARS
COSTS	CAN'T REMEMBER
BÜSSLI LOVES	HIS SAME-AGE WESTFALIA TRAILER

The interior of the Westfalia trailer also had to be restored in order to keep up with the T1 masterpiece. No sheet metal work, but solid carpentry and upholstery were needed here. The initial resentment gradually gave way to the pursuit of perfection.

Apart from partner companies specializing in retrofitting, the VW Group also had a wide range of suitable transporters for the last trip in a person's life. The Kombi was a familiar sight to every funeral guest and its luxury trims, silver bumpers, chrome hubcaps and enlarged side windows lifted the spirits a bit despite the grief. Milk glass windows and purple curtains were available at an extra charge.

Black Bay back from Corsica

This is an unsusual double cabin hearse, built in 1976 for VW by Fritz Freckinger in Augsburg. In Corsica there used to be ten of these cars which had been extended by 50 cm, but only one of them was lucky enough not to end up at the junkyard but with Pascal Amodru. „From the moment I saw it I wanted it, as it's really rare and original. I love the Porsche black and the red vinyl interior and I hope I can keep it until my very last trip in many years," says Pascal with a smile.

Crew cab Hearse

TYPE	FRICKINGER CONVERSION,
	PASCAL AMODRU, SERIAL KOMBI, F
ENGINE	NOS 1,600 CC
	DUAL CARBURETOR
HE LOVES	PORSCHE BLACK,
	RED VINYL, RESTO CALS

21-window Samba

In 1950, the production of the VW Transporter T1 starts with two units per day. From its early days to the last of the line, 1.83 million Kombis were produced. In 1951, at the first International Motor Show after the war, VW presented the first special model of the T1, the „Deluxe Microbus", for which the name „Samba" was coined. It has 23 windows and luxurious equipment. Apart from the chrome ornaments and the two-tone paint finish, the large folding sunroof is one of the reasons why the Samba is still the most popular model among collectors today. In 1963, a larger rear window was installed, giving the driver a better view out the back. The Samba loses its two corner windows and since then it is also known as the 21-window bus.

The best coffee in Tehran

Where do they make the best coffee in Tehran? Of course in a VW bus, or rather in two VW busses. If you combine a crew cab pickup with a bus without a front axle, you get a mobile semi-trailer coffee shop. Arash Arwin and the guys from the Biroon Café want to brew the best coffee in Tehran. They already have the most original coffee bar, that's for sure.

PLASTIC
WCM
WEST COAST METRIK INC.
RUBBER
VW POR
the Fatherland Tour '90

True to the company motto of West Coast Metric Inc. from Harbor City in California „We are the VW guys, we collect, restore, drive, show, race and love Volkswagen", a 1957 smashed in single cab got a second chance as a trailer. The Pearsons separated the superstructure from the chassis, made a rear fold-down ramp and welded another front panel on. Done.

Todd Pearson's Blue Pair

For WCM it all started back in 1977 with a commitment to provide the highest quality parts for VWs that would meet or if possible exceed the originals in look, feel, fit and quality. WCM is a family business and out of the wide variety of parts they manufacture for Kombis and Beetles, over 96% of those are made in California. Only the elegant black covers of the pickup and trailer are from Brazil.

Blue Pair
West Coast Metric, CA

YEAR	1957
TYPE	SINGLE CAB, FLATBED TRUCK
MADE IN	USA
BOTH LIKE	MATT BLACK, BLUE STEEL

VW Busbretta

„When my son and I drive along the streets, the passers-by crane their necks. Our trips can last forever because we are constantly being photographed," says John Dryer. This is not a rolling rubbish bin, but a sidecar for a scooter that looks a bit like a miniature VW camper. „No one has ever seen anything like it, and it's a great feeling to look into people's faces when they realize it's a miniature motorhome." It took him seven months of welding and screwing to finish this unique construction. As soon as the lights were attached to the „camper" and shining brightly, he colour-coordinated them with his Lambretta. I've been driving scooters for 27 years, for me they are the classics of locomotion and our culture here in Great Britain," he adds. I've built so many things over the years that my friends are not surprised by anything anymore," says John with a smile.

Sam’s Burger Deli and Schroeder’s

Sam Edward‘s family restaurant staff included a NASA astrophysicist, a satellite dish vendor and a retired US Marines sergeant. Harold Storey, a veteran of the Battle of the Bulge, is a regular. Just as unusual is its distinctive mark, visible from far away, a red 1961 bus on stilts with wings and a tail assembly. Everybody knows Sam‘s Burger in Rome, Georgia.

Rustyness

Samba Submarine

This 1957 Samba Deluxe bus was found underwater in a Norwegian Fjord after it had been put there in 1973, discarded because of a mere gearbox problem. Morten Lund, a passionate VW collector, sent divers down and a mini ROV sub with a camera. In 2009, the former hotel bus was recovered from a depth of 15 metres, filled with crap and some 300 full bottles of water. As it was parked face down it had frontal damage and at the rear some old stoves being dumped on it had left their marks. For Morten Lund it's not a question of whether the bus is worth restoring, but how long it'll take to get Samba back on the road. And apparently there are other old cars down there including a late 1950s VW pickup and a 1954 Beetle. You have to take your hat off to him for his determination and hardcore enthusiasm alone!

Samba Submarine
Morten Lund

YEAR	1957
TIME UNDER WATER	35 YEARS
BEST FRIEND	CRANE TRUCK
HE HATES	GLASS BOTTLES IN THE BACK
HIS DREAM	BEING PARKED PROPERLY

Splittie the hard way

Richard Kimbrough's 1961 Rustybus is an experienced mountain bus. The Shasta Snow Trip, or SST, is a unique adventure for T1 enthusiasts deep in the woods of Northern California. Half a dozen mountain passes have to be conquered and the trip also involves 450 miles on dirt roads and forest paths through mud and rivers. Only models before 1967 are admitted. The intrepid participants of the SST call themselves Newts - they love humidity as much as amphibians do. „It's only fun with old Kombis," says Justin Campbell, the initiator. „No other car brand can convey so much excitement and enthusiasm." Although Richard's Kombi has no syncro drive, it's extremely off-road capable - and the water will run off again eventually. 50 buses setting out with one goal: arriving together. That makes friendships for life.

Schlitz
Schlitznic Cooler
GPV
188C

In 1963, the Hightop Splitscreen left Wolfsburg, Germany, to become a Norwegian ambulance. When it had served its due, it finally landed in the UK in 2006 where Jason Cooper had it transformed by VW experts T2Detectives. Disk brakes and aluminium wheels were fitted, it was lowered and treated with a protective wax. Jason replaced the washable inner lining with a unique bamboo surf shack interior.

The Rustbus

Of the rare 1963 Hightop Splitscreen there are less than 50 left in the world. The Rothfink Rustbus is a real head turner, and when Jason is on the road with it, he gets waving grandmas, laughing youngsters, people shaking their heads in disbelief, thumbs up and and the same smile on everyone's face. „My kids love him, he's part of our family," says Jason. The Rustbus has won countless VW competitions including five Vanfest Trophies. He had a TV appearance on the BBC and has plenty of pictures in VW magazines around the world. For some years now, Jason's bus has mainly been driving wedding couples to the church or, the day before, the boys to the stag night. The vehicle proves fantastic for photo opportunities, with fresh tropical flowers used for every wedding.

THURLOW

Steampunk paraphernalia

Steampunk and VW busses are Steve Kay's hobbies which he combined in his 1965 „rat look" camper. The Victorian gas lamps are solar-powered, the rooftop chair and original vintage snowshoes are from the 1920s, the log burner was salvaged off an English canal boat. All the interior woodwork are scrap pieces, and the curtains and much of the brass are from scouring antique shops, car boots and salvage yards.

EOL 756C

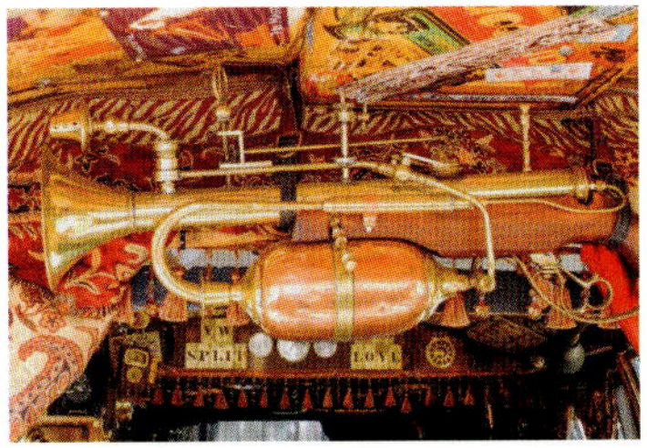

The „Steamvagon" was lowered 12" front and 10" back including tubbing the front wheelwells to adjust the van to the 17" hydro dipped radar alloys. The body colour is always changing as Steve is never happy with it for long and keeps adding hand-painted signs and pin striping. Later model disc brakes and a 1776cc high compression engine was built in to pull all the extra weight. Old snow shoes, boxes, a bird cage, hemp rope and ladders are built into the roof. The interior features 3 steampunk blunderbus rifles, 3 flintlock pistols, a revolver, a sword stick, 2 walking canes and many unique brass items, partly from Steve's own steampunk collection. „Numerous other parts, odds and sods, were scoured off the Internet. My van will never be finished, because I'm constantly evolving it some more," says Steve.

Steamvagon

Steve Kay

YEAR	1965 CAMPER VAN
HOBBY	STEAMPUNK
BEST FRIEND	DOG "KENNEL"
HE LOVES	BRASS
HIS DREAM	A ROLE IN A JULES VERNE ADAPTATION

V8 Single Cab Street Rod

The owner posted a couple of photos in which the truck had rusted in half under the drip edge of a barn. I called the owner and he asked what my plans were for it. He seemed intrigued with my answer. He told me that he and his son had purchased the truck, or what was left of it, as a father and son project. Sadly, the son passed away, so the father was looking for someone that would make something different and interesting out of it. He wanted $500 for it and offered, if I paid for the gas, to deliver it to me. I was very happy to skip the 10 hour round trip drive, so he (70) and his 71 year old friend loaded it onto the bed of his diesel dually truck and they delivered it a few days later! For endless magnificent modification details over the years check www.BenModified.com.

V8 Single Cab Street Rod

YEAR (FRONT)	1961 SINGLE CAB
ENGINE	400 HP SMALL BLOCK
	CHEVY 350 MID ENGINE
INTERIOR	VERY BASIC
HE LOVES	BULL HORNS
HIS DREAM	A REAL T1 REAR END

Two uncles and a nephew

In his home country Namibia, Eric Sell, a.k.a. EES, not only produces music and videos, but also zebra skin shoes, hot spices and power drinks. With the help of two uncles, he occasionally cleans the Namib Desert of VW busses which have been deserted or are being improperly used to keep animals in. „I just can't leave them behind, even if sometimes there's nothing left apart from the handbrake lever."

Ees

In the past few years, EES participated in all VW bus contests and raffles to make his dream come true of a trip through Germany in a Kombi. Pallets of chocolate bars, soft drinks, salads and sausages were put away at parties, empty bottles were perused in beverage shops and friends were forced to go shopping to get hold of the sought-after codes in lids and on packaging. In 2017, the effort and perseverance paid off, a T2a/b is ready for cruising in Germany. „Eric should be two, really," says his uncle about his nephew's energy and inventiveness, „but I think it's great: If he is set on doing something, no one can stop him."

With plenty of spare parts and tools, the trio hits the road with the oldies. The main thing is that the Kombi is back on wheels and can be pulled home with an all-wheel drive Beetle with a slightly tuned engine. Up to 1,700 km are ahead of them, which makes it even more fun for the family, forcing them to spend the nights in safari camps with extended barbecues under the starry sky.

K ER 571

„Sensational oldtimer discovery in Beuel“ was the unusual title of an article in the local press. Can this pile of rusted metal be turned into a Samba bus again? Some may well have had their doubts. Not so the new owner, who looks optimistically into the Samba future and takes all the time necessary for a careful restoration. Perfectly matching the laid-back 24.5 hp in the rear.

The oldest Samba in the world

„For someone like me who has been working with VW buses for 30 years, this is like the Holy Grail. Such an early Samba is like the Blue Mauritius,“ says Florian Kalff from Bonn. It could well be the oldest Samba in the world. Found and dug out on a pasture in the Eifel, the chassis number shows that this is the second underbody from the first year of production 1951. The last vehicle inspection sticker points to a decommissioning in 1961. That year, the engine power was increased from 24.5 to 34 hp and a synchronized gearbox was installed. At the time, certainly an argument to discard the „old“ Samba. Florian Kalff, a VW parts dealer and Kombi specialist, has uncovered and carefully removed component parts, engine, transmission and front axle - even some of the coveted Plexiglas skylights - from under the partly completely corroded metal sheets. The restoration he is planning can take five to ten years. Experienced coachbuilders will reconstruct missing parts and visibly include as many finds as possible. The result is intended to be a historical document and not a shiny illusion.

The “Special eight-seater model”

YEAR	1951
ENGINE	24.5 HP
INTERIOR	MISSING
HE LOVES	NEW PLEXIGLASS
HE NO LONGER LIKES	EIFEL PASTURES

Streamliner

Kieft & Klok

TYPE	VAN
EXTERIOR	FIRST PAINTWORK!
HE LOVES	CRT TELEVISION SETS, SURROUND SOUND
HE DISLIKES	JAPANESE VANS, ONLINE SHOPS

Streamliner

The bus proudly displays the traces of a long, hard-working life on its bodywork. The stripes have faded, but they still show the streamlined shape as an expression of optimism and faith in the future. The man from „Capital Service Co." used to be eagerly awaited - after all, he delivered the new CRT television sets in highly polished wooden cases.

Bulletproof

This patina is better than any tattoo. For years, this Samba bus was misused as a target in South America, which doesn't stop it from going out there and proudly telling its story. Its perforated sheet metal dress was left in place and preserved, and it was equipped with new, sophisticated technology. „El Invencible" - that somehow makes you think of John Wayne and Alamo.

The last Kohlruss Samba – only one survivor

In the 1950s, Kohlruss, a Vienna coachbuilder, equipped Samba buses with two additional roof windows above the driver and the passenger seats. Mark Spicer pulled the last surviving Kohlruss Samba out of the forest and lovingly restored it in 3,000 man hours. The technology was completely revamped and a 25 hp Boxer engine is tirelessly at work in the back.

A 1955 panel van pulled out of the woods

AirMapp's Kombi enthusiasts are dedicated to recovering forgotten VW buses from forests, swamps and quarries. This 1955 panel van was discovered by mushroom hunters in the woods near Chartreuse and someone is even said to have lived in it for several years. After some encouragement and a few minor repairs by the AirMappers, the van rolled into the valley on its own wheels.

Badass

TIRES
MENTAL BREAKDOWN
INTERGALACTIC
RECOVERY
DOTZ

VWPRO
56
YawningCatPhotography.com
MENTAL BREAKDOWN
INTERGALACTIC
RECOVERY
AIR SEA LOGISTICS
FAST ORANGE

Car customizing guru Wayne Allman is undoubtedly one of the best and most creative at his craft. Wayne runs the Intergalactic Custom Shop in Stratford-upon-Avon, building drag racers, hot rods and crazy customizations. And despite spending more than a decade constructing Mental Breakdown in his workshop in his spare time, he says he has no idea how much money he has poured into the project.

Mental Breakdown Dragster

Behind the cabin of a 1965 VW Split Screen pickup truck, on a tubular chassis, is a 8.4 litre Keith Black Hemi V8 unit that runs on methanol producing an incredible 2,000 hp. „It does 0-150 mph in four seconds, that's violent. It pulls about 2.5 Gs off the line and the same negative Gs when the parachutes open," says Wayne with his typical grin. He really loves what he does.

Mental Breakdown
Intergalactic Custom SHOP
Wayne Allman

YEAR	1965 FLATBED TRUCK
ENGINE	8.4 L KEITH BLACK V8
COMPRESSOR	2,000 HP
¼ MILE	7.1 S @ 315 KM/H
HE LOVES	METHANOL AND HIS BRAKE PARACHUTES

Fluffy

is a Volkswagen T1 monster truck owned by Kevin King from Waycross, Georgia. It is sponsored by the comic Gabriel Iglesias (a.k.a. Fluffy) and made its debut in 2006 in Birmingham, Alabama, replacing King's famous Strait Jacket. Kevin's 8.4 litre BBC engine needs plenty of methanol to breathe. Fluffy is therefore the only alcoholic with a hydraulic all-wheel steering and shoes that are 170 cm high and 110 cm wide.

Fluffy
The Monster Truck

YEAR	1963
CONSTRUCTOR	KEVIN KING
ENGINE	8.4 L BIG BLOCK CHEVY V8
SHOES	4 TIMES 168 X 109 CM
HE LOVES	METHANOL FLIPS
HE DISLIKES	LOWRIDERS

Perry Watkins is a true Brit and has created a number of bizarre vehicles, including a 19" Batmobile replica called „Flatmobile" and „Wind Up", the smallest car in the world and the size of a washing machine. Since 2010, he holds another world record for the fastest piece of furniture in the world - a car made from a dining table and chairs. His latest creation is a Rolls Royce jet engine mounted on a VW platform truck.

Oklahoma Willy Jet Split

YEAR	1963 / JET 1986
ENGINE	ROLLS-ROYCE VIPER
	535 TURBOJET
POWER	5,000 HP
CONSUMPTION	38 L/MIN
¼ MILE	12.2 S @ 212 KM/H

Oklahoma Willy

Perry found the 1958 VW flatbed pickup on a farm in Oklahoma. Now it's not carting straw anymore, but has an ultra-powerful 5,000 hp jet engine on its bed, for speeds of over 400km/h. „I had no idea how the car would react, after all it's 60 years old and as aerodynamic as a brick. With the enormous thrust it could get out of control, tip over or even flip. But it worked out perfectly, and with the jet propulsion in my back I felt like I had been strapped onto a giant firework rocket," says Perry. He now hopes that Oklahoma Willy will be recognized by Guinness World Records as the world's strongest road vehicle.

„**Volkswagen buses** have always been the epitome of freedom," says Strawn in his 1960s style office. After discovering Walter, he put together the legendary „Walter Tribe Team" and jointly they reconfigured Walter to his current size. Walter is still saving lives in his own way, today he's saving people from boredom.

Walter The Bus

Walter, the world's largest VW bus began his life in 1963 as an airport rescue vehicle. 50 years later, Kirk Strawn transformed the 23 window bus. The 2:1 scale replica of a classic Kombi stands for the values of the VW bus culture: freedom, mobility, peace, cooperation, community and creativity. On his trips, Walter encourages people to dream big, live big or just enjoy the ride.

WBX Racer
Matze Schütz

YEAR	1984
ENGINE	WBX 2,600 CC; 242 HP
¼ MILE	14.2 S
HE LOVES	HIS VMAX 210 KM/
BOTH DISLIKE	FRILLS

The modifications read like the packing list for a space mission: Total weight only 1,044 kg, carbon roof skin and sliding door (5.4 kg), bumpers 500 g instead of 6 kg, connecting rod 5.5 „ light, piston 98 mm light, perforated brake discs. Everything on Matze's T3 is light, hollowed out, replaced by carbon fibre or at least perforated. „ All I need to drive is my seat, I got rid of the dashboard and the heating and I don't need the speedometer either, because I always know my speed, and carpets are totally out of place in a car," smiles Matze. „I already saved 380 kg, I'm going for a total weight of 999 kg."

Ultra light WBX Racer

Matze only has one goal: to save weight! Anything that is not absolutely necessary for driving has to go. Comfort? That's something he doesn't need. His concept is gaining speed by saving weight, not by increasing power. His garage is full of superfluous stuff already, but Matze still feels his Kombi is too heavy. The next thing will be perforating some metal sheets or rails.

Hoosier

„I wanted to build a mid-engine hot rod," says Ken. Armed with a metal saw, a welder, a borrowed bead roller and a lifetime's worth of hot rod know-how, Ken shoehorned a colossal Chevy V8 engine into a 1962 VW Type 2 Microbus. At times, on Utah highway, you will catch a glimpse of the VW in your mirror, then the dull rumble from behind turns into the thunder of 600 supercharged horses as the bus charges by.

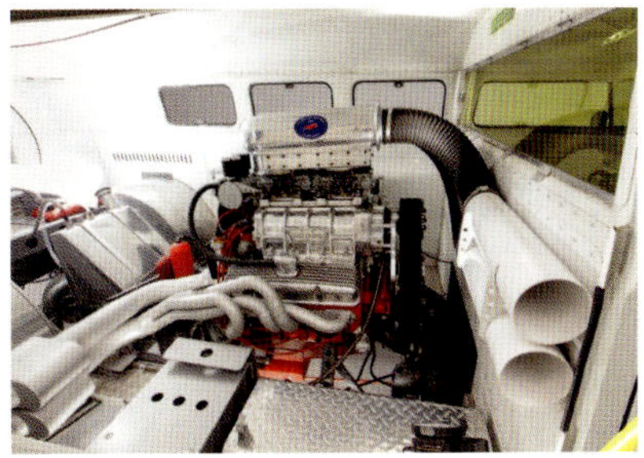

Ken Prather's Express Bus

Just about every part of this VW bus has a story and the gas pedal is no exception. „I made it from a kitchen spoon my wife gave me," says Ken with a fond smile. „I don't make any drawings, I work „from mind to metal". To lower the height, I cut the roof into six pie-shaped pieces and then I built a frame out of conduit to support the sections while I welded the whole thing back together."

Ken Prather's Express Bus

YEAR	1962
ENGINE	V8 CHEVY 5.8 L WEIAND
	TURBOCHARGER, 600 HP,
	LOWERED 18 CM
HE LOVES	HIS GULLWING DOOR
HE DISLIKES	DOOR HANDLES

Not born to run, but to live fast and ride free
Wind Split
www.serial-kombi.com
O/FF 71
OUTLAW
Go to Bonneville Salt Flats!
www.serial-kombi.com

Pascal Amodru of Serial Kombi specializes in repairs and the sale of spare parts for VW Kombis. To mark the company's 10th anniversary, Pascal and his team created a one-off drag Kombi – a high roof model. „Wind Split" is an excellent ambassador for the company. Pascal mainly used original parts and Wind Split is much more than a shell on a tubular frame with a huge engine behind the driver's seat.

Wind Split

Thanks to Pascal's driving skills and the creativity of Serial Kombi, it is one of the fastest Kombis despite the bad aerodynamics. Only the original 1.5 l four-cylinder engine with around 50 hp was replaced by a 2.3 l engine. Cylinder drilling and racing components increased the power to 230 hp and nitrous oxide pushes it up to 330 hp. Wind Split is going for 12 seconds for the quarter mile. Impressive!

Wind Split
Pascal Amodru

YEAR	1967 HIGH ROOF
ENGINE	2.3 L NITROUS OXIDE ENGINE, 330 HP
¼ MILE	12,107 S @ 179.54 KM/H
HE LOVES	AIR-COOLED ORIGINALS
HE DISLIKES	V8 BBC ENGINES

What happens when you screw together a T1, a snow groomer and a load of DJ equipment? The ultimate party rig for winter events! Created by Bernd Berger from Austria, he also uses the crawler vehicle for beach parties. As the caterpillar cannot cover long distances, a trailer takes it to the event. It can manage the last metres up the hill or down the beach and then roof up and let's party!

Snow Kombi

Basically, only the shell was left from the T1. For stability, the front doors were welded shut; the only access to the vehicle is through the gullwing doors on the right-hand side. Disc brakes on the sprockets are used for steering. The roof was cut out along its entire length and replaced by a lift-up roof made of plastic. The DJ equipment consists of 1,000 watt subwoofers, a mixer and two turntables.

Snow Kombi
Bernd Berger

YEAR	1960, ON BOMBARDIER B01 SNOW GROOMER
ENGINE	70 HP
VMAX	15 KM/H
HE LOVES	SLOPES, EASILY UP TO 60%
HE DISLIKES	HIGHWAYS

Filmore Ratrod Split Window Kombi

YEAR	1956
ENGINE	3.4 L PORSCHE TURBO, 433 HP
¼ MILE	10.5 S @ 171.6 KM/H
HE LOVES	DRAGWAY WEEKENDS
HE DISLIKES	WATER COOLING

Alder Outlaws VW Racing

The Alders are a VW mad family from near Brisbane in Australia who live, breathe, modify, rebuild and love to race Volkswagens. The nine family members of the racing team proudly united several VWs under the banner „Alder Outlaws VW Racing". The senior and star of the group is Filmore, a 1956 VW bus powered by a 3.4 litre six-cylinder turbocharged Porsche engine.

The Trippy Tippy Hippy Van

Jeff „Speedycop“ Bloch has constructed some of the most incredible vehicles in the past. For the 24 Hours of LeMons (for cars that cost no more than $500), with his Gang of Outlaws he created a sideways race car. He found a rusty 1976 Westfalia Camper rotting away on a field in Tennessee, hollowed it out and put it on its side.

Artness

Kunstmu
W 89287A

Erwin Wurm's Curry Bus

The artist Erwin Wurm transformed an original VW Kombi into a Curry Bus where original VW Currywurst is sold. Erwin Wurm is a crossover artist between sculpture and performance. With his „Fat Sculptures" the artist shows middle-class status symbols like cars or single-family homes in a `fatty´, bloated shape. Fat distorts volumes and shapes – that is what intrigues Erwin Wurm.

A Kombi in The Elixir of Love

An unusual stage design and a tumultuous production of Donizetti's opera buffa „The Elixir of Love" against the spectacular natural setting of the quarry in St. Margarethen, a firework of wit and melodies – and a Kombi in the middle of it. The stage design represents an oversized Wurlitzer jukebox with tonearm and turntable and Dulcamara drives on stage as a hippie in a VW bus.

This

Bruegel-Bosch Bus

Kim Adams' Bruegel-Bosch Bus feels like an exploded toy chest – a sculpture set in and around an old 1960 VW Transporter, stuffed with action figures and other nostalgic ephemera. Repeatedly in his work, Canadian artist Kim Adams has explored the patterns of a mobile society. Blending humour, satire and seriousness, he builds "worlds" as a means of social critique. His `Bus´ is a Kubrickesque megalopolis made of icons symptomatic in present society. The Bruegel-Bosch Bus is a visual masterpiece that appears to pull a post-industrial universe displaying a cornucopia of fantastic and seductive worlds that play with our senses. This futuristic diorama was produced over a 7-year span and presents a micro-model of North American society fixed on leisure and entertainment. Buildings from different epochs are aligned side by side and space becomes an imaginary territory where chaos prevails. In the Art Gallery of Hamilton, Ontario, overlooking the Niagara Falls, Adams is constantly refining his permanent fixture.

DUNLOP
REIFEN
Dorfstraße
EXKLUSIVE MODELLOBJEKTE
WWW.XSDREAMS.DE
FÜR AUTO- UND OLDTIMERLIEBHABER
Pepsi-Cola
VEEDOL
MOTOR OIL
55

The freelance artist and photographer Dirk Patschkowski acquired his 1965 split window pickup with 44 hp first-hand from an Italian olive grower. The velvet green and pearl white are authentic VW colours. He does many thousands of kilometres with it every year, and he also uses it to display his art. His Kombi is fully equipped: The opening Safari windscreens are the air-conditioning and the fur cover the seat heating.

XS Dreams makes dreams come true

Some have Dirk Patschkowski reproduce their own vehicle in miniature, others want to have a preview of their dream car, and many have their dream of a barn find preserved on a scale of 1:18. In the artfully composed miniature scenes everything is there, just like in a dream: the dust, the cobwebs, the bales of straw, the rusty tools, the yellowed magazines. But Dirk Patschkowski not only makes vintage car models look old, he also ventures into the patina of luxury classic cars on a 1:1 scale. Everything Dirk makes or refines is absolutely unique in terms of detail and quality. He has an incredibly good eye and a keen sense for detail. Not everything is for sale, but can be borrowed by passionate VW fans for birthdays or similar events.

Revamped

If half of it has rusted away, Martin Schlund from Endingen, Germany, takes the rest to make furniture out of it. Car furniture combines the possibilities of a unique interior design with the distinctive forms of young-timers and oldtimers, but also some new car models. People remember the distinctive forms of vehicles and they are associated with many personal memories and the lifestyle of those years. Even after more than 150 pieces of car furniture and over 200 accessories, every transformation of a rust bucket into a unique piece of car furniture is always an exciting but also labor-intensive process. Every piece of furniture takes at least 100 hours of manual labour. If he has an order and no rust bucket at his fingertips, Martin goes out and looks for one.

From the scrap yard into the living room: sitting in the engine compartment, sleeping on the platform, sideboards and shelves made of tailgates, a sofa with gullwing doors. Not a cheap, but a very individual style. And this furniture is made to last.

Markus Pajer‘s dioramas

Markus Pajer only needs about two days to let a VW Kombi go completely rusty. Then the windshield gets a crack and the tyres are flattened. Empty oil cans, dirty rags and old newspapers are placed on the front seats, and the work of art on a scale of 1:18 is finished. The cars are given an old, rusty look in elaborate manual work. The dioramas are made of wood, cement, stone, plexiglass, sheet metal and real brickwork. To make the illusion come alive, Pajer uses small everyday items such as matchboxes, magazines, tools and oil cans for his display. As a trained dental technician, he has a steady hand and the right tools. „I just need to find out as much as possible about the original. After all, you also get plastic body parts that couldn‘t rust at all.“

Wurm's Telekinetically Bent VW Van

The artist Erwin Wurm says that his telekinetically bent VW van was created with the help of a guru from India who insisted on a business class ticket from India and $2,000. In addition, the artist and his assistants had to help mentally bend the bus. Warped in the middle by a 30-degree bend between its two axles, with its wheels straight, this bus would go in a circle forever.

A whole new ball game

The T-Ball looks like a gondola for a single passenger. Lars Erik Fisk condenses the form and characteristics of the original into a concise and humorous ball whose aesthetics fascinate the viewer. He compressed a 1960 Volkswagen bus into a VW ball to transform it into a sphere, thus capturing its essence and, of course, everyone recognizes the VW Kombi.

The Pack

The tailgate of a 1961 VW bus is open and 24 wooden sledges, arranged side by side in three rows in opposite direction to the vehicle, seem to be tumbling from the back of the van. Each sledge carries a lump of fat, a torch and a roll of felt strapped on with a belt. Only one sledge differs from the others in the mirror-image arrangement of the equipment. The members of this pack do not come as friends, but as invaders resolutely marching forward. In the historical context of 1969, this is a political statement of both sensual and meaningful power. „The Pack": It stands for the invasion of the Americans in Vietnam, the use of police force against students, the invasion of Warsaw Pact troops into the CSSR, the actions of the Italian police against workers. According to Beuys' own statement, the survival kit on each sledge represents „orientation, nutrition and warmth, i. e. what one needs in extreme conditions and at the lowest level to ensure survival." In any case, this is another invaluable T1 from 1961.